DIGITAL CUPID

How to Find Your Match Online

CARRIE DICKIE

DIGITAL CUPID: How to Find Your Match Online

Published by Pure Joy Press
San Juan Capistrano, CA

Copyright © 2023 by Carrie Dickie. All rights reserved.

No part of this book may be reproduced in any form or by any mechanical means, including information storage and retrieval systems without permission in writing from the publisher/author, except by a reviewer who may quote passages in a review.

All images, logos, quotes, and trademarks included in this book are subject to use according to trademark and copyright laws of the United States of America.

ISBN: 978-0-9974590-3-6

RELATIONSHIPS / Dating

All rights reserved by Carrie Dickie and Pure Joy Press.

Printed in the United States of America.

CONTENTS

Introduction	v
1. Laying the Groundword	1
2. The Profile	23
3. My Profile	35
4. Connecting	39
5. The Date	51
6. When The Sparks Don't Fly	55
7. A Few Of My Dates	59
8. Resources and Inspiration	65
9. Last Thoughts	71
Free Offer	77
About the Author	79

INTRODUCTION

So, you want to spend your life with another human being but navigating the whole dating thing while juggling a job and commitments seems impossible. Maybe you have been married and divorced like at least 50 percent of the people out there, most of whom intended to stay married forever. Perhaps you are a widow or widower, and your marriage contract was cut short by an accident, an illness, or even suicide. You may have yet to find your match. Whether divorced, widowed, or just haven't found Mr. or Mrs. Right, this book is for you. I can help you find whatever it is you seek. Why? Because I was looking too. And, by the way, I never thought I would be. I thought I would be married for the rest of my life. I thought I would grow old with my former husband. I thought we would make

INTRODUCTION

it "till death do us part," but we didn't make it. One day we were a couple. The next day I was traveling alone. Within a few days of our separation, I realized I had a little girl inside me who had never grown up. I had lots and lots of inner work to do. I had lessons to learn, and I was terrified of being alone. It was very uncomfortable. It was utterly foreign to me not to have my "person." After intense personal inquiry, professional therapy, and enough time, I found a new "normal." I healed my inner child and became independent. I learned how to be comfortable in my skin without being part of a couple. I figured out how to be alone but not lonely.

Then, I joined the world of online dating. For fourteen months, I treated my experience as a part-time job. And oh, my goodness, I learned a lot! I talked with nearly one hundred people, many on the phone and about a third of those in person. I learned how to step into my power, remain unattached to the results, and minimize my hurt feelings and those of the men who were kind enough to meet me. I learned how to communicate fully and graciously, and eventually reached the point where I trusted my gut. I became an EXPERT! No kidding.

I have lots of insights and suggestions about what to do, and perhaps more importantly, what not to do. I know how to streamline the process. I can help you avoid wasting time on long, expensive dates when the

INTRODUCTION

interest is not mutual. I know how to avoid hurt feelings (mostly), how to tell the whole truth, nothing but the truth, so help me, God!

I fell and got back up. I laughed and cried. I got excited and terribly disappointed. And then, when I least expected it, I found love. I can help you find it too. I wrote this book because ***it is what I needed*** while going through the excruciating process of rebuilding my life after the divorce. This book was downloaded to me (Thank you God!), making it easier for those walking on the same path I have traveled. You'll need to commit to the following three things for the best chance of success:

1. Let go of a time frame.
2. Become familiar with the concept of nonattachment.
3. Learn to communicate.

You won't be committing to me, by the way. You will be committing to yourself. You will open the door and the windows so the light can come in and find you.

First, let go of a time frame. You are not in charge of when your perfect mate will show up. You cannot control how it will happen. You cannot determine how many dates you will go on before finding love. Your only job is to show up repeatedly, follow through with your

INTRODUCTION

commitments, and do the work. Finding a partner online will require faith.

Second, you will have to become intimately familiar with nonattachment. I wish someone had told me about the concept of nonattachment, as it pertained to the dating world, before I began my journey. It would have saved me so much anxiety and disappointment. Let me explain it by using a metaphor. Have you ever walked by a pond and watched two ducks fighting? Animals get it. They get in there and have a good tumble lasting about twenty seconds before they are done. They swim away, feathers ruffled, then raise themselves out of the water and flap like crazy. They are complete. They swim off with the elegance of a swan and never look back. They are calm. They reboot and move on.

Dogs are the same. My pup and I frequent a dog beach and repeatedly see this happen. Two dogs will get into a short skirmish. Within a few seconds, they growl, snarl, and bark, exert a ton of energy, and then move away. They shake their bodies rigorously, and they finish. They don't look back. They don't hang onto the irritation or analyze the event. It's over, and they move forward. We can learn many things by watching animals, but I digress! You cannot be attached to the outcome of any date. You are on a mission. Your job is to have fun and find your partner. Please keep it simple, and don't ruminate after the fact.

INTRODUCTION

Third, I encourage you to take this time to learn how to communicate. It's excellent practice to express your feelings with total strangers. This will prepare you for when it really matters. Most people are like you. They are looking for company, friendship, companionship, or even love. They are putting themselves out there just like you are. They are taking risks, and many are laying their hearts on the line. Now is a perfect time to be yourself. Be authentic. Be who you are and allow others to do the same. Online dating can help you grow if you let it.

In summary, let go and let God, don't be attached to the results, and grow yourself. Your success with online dating will be in direct proportion to the energy you invest. I promise you will get out what you put in. Do the work. You're worth it! So, get ready, get set, let's GO! I am excited to share what I learned.

Chapter One

LAYING THE GROUNDWORD

DETERMINE WHAT YOU WANT

What do you want to bring into your life? Do you want to marry? Do you want to be in a committed, long-term relationship? Do you want to see who's out there and have some fun? Are you looking for a friend to hang out with? Anything and everything goes as long as you are clean and clear. Yes, that's right. You have to tell the truth. And the first person you must be honest with is yourself. What do you want? You may not know precisely what you want, so you must date some people to figure it out. It's time to do some soul-searching. Only you know why you picked up this book. Let's get started!

Deciding what you want is serious business. We live in a creative universe and have the power to magnetically pull others toward us, especially if we believe we do. The more seriously you take this step, the more efficient and effective you will be in attracting the mate you have been dreaming of. So, let's do this!

Get up right now and grab three things. First, get some paper. It may be notebook paper, printer paper, or something more beautiful if you are the artsy type. The universe won't care what you choose, but it may be more desirable to you, and this is what's important right now. It would be best to feel good while determining what you want in a wife, husband, friend, partner, or lover. While you're up, grab some scissors and a "vessel." Choose a bag, a box, a vase, a jar, or anything that can hold the bits of paper you will write on. Now, either cut up the piece of paper or tear it artistically. Do whatever excites you about creating the person you will spend your time with. You will have a bunch of small bits of paper sitting in front of you. Now get ready to create! Sit down, get comfortable, and close your eyes. We are going to clear your mind, heart, and spirit. It's time to change gears and let everything else exit the building so you can make room for something new to enter.

Take a huge deep breath on a count of five (one . . . two . . . three . . . four . . . five). Hold it at the top for a count of five (one . . . two . . . three . . . four . . . five) and let it out for a count of five (one . . . two . . . three . . . four . . . five). Now relax to the count of five (one . . . two . . .

three . . . four . . . five). Do this repeatedly until you start to feel the tension leaving, at least five or six times. DO NOT SKIP THIS PART! You are beginning the creative process, and being clean, clear, and relaxed is critical. Hang out for a moment and start to dream! Don't overthink.

Create a picture in your mind's eye. Physical characteristics may or may not be super important to you, but it's an easy place to start. Most of us will agree on the significance of chemistry. When I was dating online, I saw that word all the time. People talked about wanting to feel attracted to their partners. We are human beings, and energy is fundamental. Physical attraction isn't everything, but it certainly is something! Let's begin by conjuring up your partner in your imagination. What would you like your perfect companion to look like? What is the feature that attracts you? Is it a smile? The eyes? A person's teeth? Their hair? See them clearly and write them down. Here are some examples:

- Big, bright smile
- Expressive eyes
- Long, dark hair
- Muscular legs
- Strong hands

Pick up a piece of paper and write to get comfortable with the process. Have fun with this, and don't think about it too much. Just go.

Part of knowing what you want is knowing what you *don't* want. Only write things down that you *do* want. For example, don't write "not too thin" if you prefer a person with a bigger build. Don't write "not too tall" if you like a shorter woman. You attract what you focus on, so determine precisely what feature you want. Be as clear, concise, and detailed as you can. As you write down the features you like, you will begin to feel excited about the person you are attracting. Enjoy this essential part of the process! Some may think that beauty is only skin deep and that this part of the process is superficial. I get it. We are just warming up. Keep writing on your scraps of paper. Start from the tip of the head to the tip of the toes. We are practicing for the big stuff to come! I'm going to share some of the things on my list to give you ideas:

Physically fit: I was a fitness instructor and a personal trainer in my twenties and thirties. I have been into health and wellness my whole life. I juice fruits and veggies every day and drink clean, pure water. I love yoga, hiking, and cycling, so my special someone needed to care about keeping his body healthy and strong from the inside out. Healthy eating was also on my list. Since I love to cook and prepare healthy foods, I wasn't much interested in a picky eater who wouldn't appreciate those food choices.

A lovely chest was really important to me. I love a hairy, developed chest to lay my face in. Just sayin'. I'm sitting on my bed right now looking through a mountain of pieces of paper, and I cannot find many that list physical characteristics, but there are a few, and a hairy chest is at the top of my list. Nice legs are there as well. Hairy, tanned, and athletic is the way I like them.

Feel it as you write down what you want. It's supposed to be FUN! When I thought about how I wanted to determine height, I couldn't get a clear vision, so I wrote "Perfect height." I am so glad I did. I got exactly what I didn't even know I wanted! If unclear, name the characteristic and write, "Perfect _____ for me!" I did that a few times and was blessed and excited about what God, the universe, and my angels brought to me. They know what is highest and best if we are willing to turn over the reins and ask.

Let's continue. Close your eyes and start to envision the lifestyle you want to make with your partner. What do you enjoy doing in your spare time? Do you like to ride your bike by the beach? Do you love to hike in the mountains? Do you enjoy playing board games and cooking at home? Create a movie in your mind about what your perfect weekend might look like. Would you want to dress up and go out to dinner? Would you prefer relaxing at home with a good book or Netflix movie? Determine who you are and what you enjoy to attract someone who can sit alongside you. Feel engaged in each activity you write on your scraps of paper. Here are a few of the things I wrote on mine:

- Loves to hike
- Loves to read
- Loves to watch the stars at night
- Loves the outdoors and nature
- Loves the ocean and the beach
- Cyclist or better (Maybe there is a new sport I would love that I'm not engaged in now. Keep the door open for something new you might enjoy!)

Doing this exercise up front will create clarity and purpose in your search. You will consider all this as you scan profiles and exchange text messages, emails, and phone calls. Additionally, you can quickly and easily create your profile since you worked hard to determine what you seek.

Now it's time to get more detailed. What character traits do you want in your mate? What is important to you when considering a person's insides? I spent 80 percent of my time here. The more time you spend, the better. Like at a restaurant, you are ordering with God and the universe. Would you ask the server to bring you whatever they wanted? I have heard a few people do it in my life but it's not my style. If you do choose to leave it to God, then great! And the law of attraction is real. It will still be enormously beneficial to envision what you want. Here goes! Let me share some of the things I had on my list:

- Loves children and animals
- Loves to laugh
- Honest
- Patient
- Kind
- Giant, open heart
- Gracious
- Friendly to everyone he meets
- Healthy relationship with social media
- Healthy relationship with alcohol
- Healthy family relationships
- Emotionally available
- Financially responsible

Now, stop reading my list and think more about yours. The more energy you expend here, the more clarity you will receive, and the more intensely you will be able to attract what you want. Consider this while envisioning: Finding a mate is like painting a room. It's all in the prep work. If you don't cover the floor, mask and tape the ceiling, and carefully choose the colors you want, you will make a mess. Take the time to thoroughly examine what will benefit you, and you will be more likely to draw it to you.

Let me tell you about my friend Cherise. I met her at a business meeting nearly thirty years ago. I saw her in front of me in her sharp, red suit and heard her laughter. I thought, "I have to get to know this girl. She's fun!" We became fast friends and business partners, and I watched Cherise create her husband. No kidding. She would look up and say, "I wonder where my future husband is right now. I wonder what he's doing. Carrie, he is funny. He makes me laugh. He is financially fit but you would never know it. He is Greek like me, and we will go to church together. My future husband is my best friend." For a year, I heard her describe him again and again, in detail, and watched her smile and laugh and visualize him in her mind's eye. It was phenomenal! Cherise finally met Ron when the little old Greek man at church set them up on a blind date. I have watched them laugh together, cry, grow, have three children, and build their lives. Ron is everything Cherise described before ever having laid eyes on him!

Now let me tell you another story about Cherise. She grew up in Lancaster with her parents and three siblings. She left home to attend UC Irvine and leased an apartment near the campus. She shared space with three other girls, one living in her room. I watched Cherise for two years. She was either running an ad for a roommate, kicking one out of the apartment, cleaning up someone else's mess, or trying to collect the rent. It was a full-time job! It didn't occur to me then, but it seems crystal clear today that Cherise forgot to determine exactly what she wanted. She could have asked for three roommates who were polite, considerate, fiscally responsible, and long-term. Instead, Cherise had seventeen roommates in the four years she attended college and a lot of hassle. Please remember these two stories as you prepare to look for your match.

Be thorough in your examination of what you want in a partner. Take your time and cover everything. Here are some other things I had in my beautiful box that was so much fun to open as I read my bits of paper repeatedly throughout the four years it took to meet my match.

- Good dresser
- Smells good
- Has healthy family relationships
- Authentic
- Practices self-care
- Self-aware
- Loves adventure

- Trustworthy
- Peaceful sleeper (Notice I didn't say, "doesn't snore." That's NOT what I want, so I didn't focus on that. I focused on what I WANTED . . . a peaceful sleeper!)
- Well-adjusted
- Observant
- Loves to eat!
- Romantic
- Present
- Supportive
- Nontraditional
- Sexually healthy
- Good communicator
- Well-spoken
- Fun
- Open at the top
- Seeker
- Loyal
- Practices nonattachment
- Altruistic
- Interesting
- Hardworking
- Good sense of humor
- Monogamous

My sweet daddy won't love this story, but I must share it because it will help you. I know his intentions were pure when we had this conversation. Shortly after my divorce, I created a list of what I wanted in a man if I ever chose to be in a partnership again. I took my time and thought about what I wanted and why it was vital for me to create it. I was excited to share my list with my dad. It took me five minutes to read it, and there was silence when I finished. Then he said, "Honey, you will be lucky if you get 50 percent of that!" I didn't get mad, and I didn't feel disappointed. I knew he was in protection mode and didn't want me to get my hopes up. His words strengthened my resolve. I decided, then and there, that I would rather be alone than settle for anything less than what was on my list. It crystallized my desire!

I am about to share the most critical point in determining what you want. Your box's last piece of paper must read, "Or something of equal value or better." What an excellent idea to invite God into your heart and soul. Acknowledging that GOD KNOWS BEST is paramount. The universe has your back. We can all use a little divine intervention, and this is the sure way to get it.

Wow! What an insurance policy if you choose to check in, listen, and follow the guidance that you receive!

Last thing on this topic. You have visualized the time you will spend with your partner. You have imagined what it will feel like to be in their company. Let's complete the final step of this part of the process. Find something yummy smelling in your home. It could be perfume or cologne. It could be a room or body spray. I chose a few essential oils that I love. Spray each piece of paper with a fragrance that is pleasing to you. Take one, last, deep breath and seal the vision in your mind and spirit. Intentionally reread each piece of paper, put it into your vessel, and close it up.

Congratulations! You have finished part one —"Determine What You Want." This step is huge. It is vital. Knowing what you want, need, and deserve is crucial to finding your match online!

CREATE THE VISION

What will your life look like when your partner arrives on the scene? Woo-HOOOO!!!! This next bit will be fun! And it can take as little as ten minutes. If you have more time than that, please allow it. It will help you. What will you FEEL like when your partner is with you? Will you go to the movies, browse at an art festival, or cuddle on the couch with some Ben and Jerry's? Maybe all of the above? Close your eyes and take those deep breaths we talked about. Breathe in for five, hold your breath at the top, breathe out for five, and hold for five at the bottom. Do it again and again until you are relaxed and present. Start to envision yourself living life with your partner. See it!

Go even deeper now. Imagine what it will feel like when you are hanging out with your partner. Will you have lunch on a sunny patio with a crisp bottle of white wine, sharing your most intimate thoughts? Are you hiking in the mountains with the wind in your hair and the birds chirping all around? Are you walking in Costco, hand in hand, discussing menus and buying toothpaste, toilet paper, and dish soap? Are you loving that you are doing it together rather than alone? INVEST some time here. The amount of energy you put into this step will directly correlate with your ability to attract what you desire.

Where will you live? Will you have an apartment or condo that you can lock up and leave for the weekend? Or will you have a home with a yard, flowers, and a garden that you plant and tend together? Will you listen to music or keep it serene and quiet? Will you have a house full of kids playing Ping-Pong and skateboards making noise outside? Will your home smell delicious because you're baking brownies and preparing for guests or a family meal? Now is your time to DREAM. You have an opportunity to imagine the life you want for yourself. Go all in. Enjoy this experience. Now is not the time to dwell on the fact that this life is not here yet. It's the time to celebrate and to feel wonderful because it has arrived, and you have cocreated it with God, the angels, and the universe at your service. At the end of your meditation, remember to add, "Or something of equal value or better." It's essential to keep the door open. I cannot tell you how many times I thought I wanted something and later realized that it was not what would have made me happy. I have prayed many prayers of gratitude for not receiving what I thought I wanted. I bet you have too!

You have envisioned the life you want with the partner of your creation. Next, let's talk about how to bring it to you. Get that pen and a bunch of paper scraps. Find another vessel and come back to me!

BECOME

Determining what you want was fun, right? It was easy once you got the ball rolling. This next part may be less fun, but it is equally as important, if not more so. Here's why. You have been clear about what you want. You have written it down. You have placed an order with the universe. You have asked God and your angels to help you find your partner. You have felt joy, excitement, and anticipation as you visualized the life you will lead with your match. Now it's time to take a good look at yourself.

How do you measure up when you think of this remarkable person with whom you will spend your time? Are you someone with the qualities a man or woman of this caliber would seek? How are you doing in that department if you are looking for a patient person? Are you patient yourself? How is your fitness regimen going if you are looking for a healthy and fit partner? If you are interested in finding a kind and compassionate mate, it may be vital that you, too, are kind and understanding. Practice being the person you are dreaming of. After all, "like attracts like," right?

Who do you need to become to attract what you want? This self-examination stuff is tricky. If you haven't done it before, you may find it challenging until you get the hang of it. If you are about ready to skip this part and jump into the next chapter, take a breath and consider the following: What if you attract the perfect mate and you are not ready to receive this fantastic person? What if you have not become the kind of man or woman this person would choose? This is tremendously important. I wanted someone confident and independent who could stand on his own two feet and handle the life he had created for himself without using substances, blaming others, or becoming emotionally disconnected. Unfortunately, I was needy, super dependent, and scared to death of being alone for the rest of my life. I had never spent any time on my own. I had gone from my parent's home to college and then from one boyfriend to another until I met and married my former husband. Let me stray a bit from the task at hand to nail this point down for you.

I was a twenty-seven-year-old college graduate who had just broken off my relationship with a serious boyfriend of three years. The counselor listened to my story and shared her professional opinion with empathy and compassion for the lost young lady that I was. She told me to take one year of my life and to spend it alone. I was to figure out who I was, what I liked, what I didn't like, and what I wanted to create. She suggested I didn't date at all for that short period. The assignment was, essentially, to spend an entire year "adulting." That day I told her, "You are right. I need to do this, and I'm going to. I need to figure out who the heck I am!" I left excited and invigorated and a teeny bit terrified. A whole year? It seemed daunting and next to impossible! I was afraid. I promptly moved on with my life without revisiting the details of the session.

I met my former husband a week later. I returned to the counselor for my session and told her I was good to go. I didn't need her anymore. I had met the man of my dreams and would likely get married soon! I never did what she suggested. I never took that year, or even a few months, to figure out who I was or what I wanted. I jumped right back into my comfort zone, and my former husband and I tied the knot just over a year later. We were together for twenty-six years.

I was used to being accountable; first to my parents, then to boyfriends, and then to my spouse. For my entire life I had been used to reporting on daily events including my studies, work, children, and events like car accidents, speeding tickets, outings with friends, and other life stuff. For twenty-six years I had another half. Getting married kept me right where I wanted to be—in my comfort zone.

When my marriage ended, I was still a child. I was twelve years old on the inside. I was like a baby who never learned to "self-soothe." We created two kids, a home, a history, and a life, but we did not get to the end of the road together. The breakup was excruciating for both of us. It wasn't fair to me, and it wasn't fair to the man with whom I spent that time. It was difficult on our boys. Here's the moral of this story: Take time for introspection. Don't pass "Go." Do NOT collect $200. It will make you better. It will grow you.

Now, grab your scrap paper and pen, and start listing the characteristics and qualities of a person who could attract the partner you envisioned. Be fearless as you take this personal moral inventory. If you crave monogamy in your relationship, have you been monogamous? If you want someone interested in growth and personal development, have you been open at the top, and willing to learn and grow? If you wish to attract someone courageous and tenacious, won't you need to be brave as well? Breathe in. Hold for five counts. Breathe out for five, and relax to the count of five. Make this list, spray the papers with an essential oil or fragrance that inspires you, visualize yourself in high vibration, and put everything into the second vessel. In the days, weeks, and months to come, you will open up these vessels, one at a time, and visualize your partner and yourself. This is your work if you choose to work it. Add passion, enthusiasm, and belief to the mix, and you cannot fail.

CLEAN UP

Hopefully, you got clarity on what you want in a partner. You likely have visualized what it will feel like when this person comes to you. You figured out who you need to become to attract what you want. I will ask you to go just a bit deeper, and I believe it will make a huge difference in your journey to find your match online. Before you create a profile, I suggest you identify and clean up your wounds. I seriously considered skipping this part because I wanted this book to be light and fun. And I promise you, we'll get back to the fun stuff once we get through this section. However, if I didn't take the time to share the following information, I feel that I would be doing you a grave disservice. I should have done this before I got married. The pain of my parent's divorce was so massive that I compressed it into a ball and shoved it down into my soul as far as possible. I was in college and had no time to deal with the total decimation of my family. I completely disconnected from my pain. It had to do with self-preservation. I couldn't stop feeling the shame, the loss, and the grief. I tucked it away for years and carried it right into my own marriage. If I had done the cleanup before I got married, I might have been able to go the distance with my former husband. Doing the heavy lifting now will help you make better choices as you navigate the online journey to finding love.

Really look at yourself. I'm not talking about the mirror. Self-reflection is critical as you consider the prospect of choosing a partner. We are human beings, and most feel better in our comfort zones. If you are coming out of a relationship and don't stop to identify what part you played in its demise, you will choose the same again. You will re-create what has just ended. Whether you left the relationship or were left behind, even in death, ask yourself these questions and be fearless in answering them:

What was beautiful about my former relationship, and what was not? How did I contribute to the not-so-great part of the relationship? What could I have done better? What could I have done differently?

You may be saying, "My partner was a creep. I did nothing to deserve the treatment I received. It wasn't about me. It was about her." I get it. It's hard to stop, drop, and look at how you may have contributed to a relationship breakdown. But the only thing worse than a breakup is another one that looks shockingly similar to the first. Ouch. Taking the time to reflect may save you time, money, and heartache.

Let's make it easy. Close your eyes again. Take a deep breath. Count to five. Hold it at the top for five. Release the breath for five, and pause at the bottom for five. Do this several more times. Find some peace in your heart and mind and consider this challenge:

You are 99 percent right. Your former partner is 99 percent wrong. I'm only asking you to give up 1 percent. You are nearly perfectly right, and they are almost perfectly wrong. Feel that. Now, with courage and conviction, because this will help you, search your heart for the 1 percent you have given up to your former partner. What tiny little 1 percent can you honestly say you could have improved on? Where could you have made a little more effort? Where could you have been a bit more patient? At what point did you start losing yourself in the relationship? When did you try too hard to become what you thought your partner wanted you to be? When did you begin to abandon yourself? When did you become incongruent? When did you fall out of alignment with your own values and morals? In what teeny tiny way did you contribute to the demise of your relationship? If you can nail this down, and I believe you can, then focus on it. Consider it. Ponder it. Own it. Stay here for a few more minutes and expand it. You may feel pain. Your heart may hurt. A wound you have been trying to outrun, shove down, or deny may surface. I invite you to embrace it. Linger there and engage with the feelings that are emerging. Allow this stuff to come up and unite with it for a moment. Spend the time you need, and let it flow through you. Please don't ignore it. Don't fight it. Don't judge it. Just feel it, flow it, and release it. Let the pain leave your physical body, and it will set you free. Remember, it takes two to have a friendship, romance, marriage, and a breakup. There are always two sides to a story, even considering cases of adultery, drug use, financial ruin, and even death. If you are fearless and take a serious look at your part in the dance, you may learn something you can take with you moving forward. Or, you may identify something you need to leave behind.

And make sure to give yourself time. Many people rush into the next relationship. Some go from one relationship to the next without any time at all in between.

Good job. You are clear on what you want. You are prepared to invest time and energy to create and receive it. You have figured out who you need to become to attract the person of your dreams and have taken inventory. You have clarified what you could have done better in your past relationships to be more aware of unhealthy patterns and habits that won't serve you in the future. I will end this conversation here. However, I would like to give you fair warning. If you skip this part, it may be problematic for you. I promise, if you don't take the time to do this work, it may come back to bite you! Enough said.

Let's move on. Now we are ready to create your profile. We are going to have FUN, FUN, FUN!

Chapter Two

THE PROFILE

I remember the night a few years ago when a friend began to share her dating experiences with me. My initial response was, "Yuk, I cannot imagine trying to date again at the ripe old age of fifty-seven!" She told me about the men chatting her up and divulged details about the conversations she was having with them. She showed me her profile, and we played on the dating app. She shared pictures and I got inquisitive. After our talk that night, I opened the app and decided to make a profile for fun. I would not participate, but at least I could get a feel for what was "out there." I asked myself, "What would I want someone to know about me? What would I need to share to attract what I want and need in a relationship?" Once I got started, I had fun! I browsed through my photos and looked for pictures that told the story of my life. I chose pics of my kids and me. I decided on photos highlighting my interest in the outdoors. I showed cycling pics, pictures of myself in nature, and photos with my girlfriends and family. I ensured that my profile reflected my passion, enthusiasm for life, love of people, and new experiences. I got into it when I started to write about who I was, where I had been, what I was looking for in a partner, and why I was on an online dating site in the first place. In one hour, I had a profile I was proud of and excited about. I was all in!

Now it's your turn! It's time to write the profile to attract the person with whom you'd like to spend your time. Let's get back to the breathing. Close your eyes again. Take a deep breath. Count to five. Hold it at the top for five. Release the breath for five, and pause at the bottom for five. Do this several more times.

WRITING YOUR PROFILE

Ask yourself the following questions and listen to your heart for the answers.

- Who am I?
- Where have I been for the last bunch of years?
- What are my goals?

- Whom do I hope to attract with this profile?
- What do I want to get out of the online dating experience?
- How do I want to share myself with people who are online looking for a partner?
- What do I want a potential date to know about me?
- Do I want them to know what I do for work?
- Do I want to share my hobbies and interests?
- Do I want them to know I am a parent?
- Do I want them to know that I am a social person, or that I enjoy spending lots of time alone?

Be sure to include details about what you are looking for. After reading your profile, a prospective date should have a pretty clear vision of who you are and what you are looking for in a partner. Think of it like a résumé. It's sort of like being an employer looking for the perfect employee. You are sharing your journey and your history, dreams and desires, and hoping to find someone who has similar wishes and goals. I suggest you put some time and energy into creating this profile. It will do the heavy lifting for you as people sift and sort and figure out if you are someone they would like to meet.

Be honest with yourself and the courageous souls putting themselves out there looking for companionship, friendship, or even love. Tell the truth. Be authentic in your profile and with your pictures. I cannot tell you how many men told me horror stories. They spoke of women posting images that were hugely outdated and nonrepresentative of their appearance. That never made sense to me. Why would a woman subject herself to the shock and awe that a man most assuredly feels when her pictures show her to be a size 6 or 8, but she shows up in person four sizes larger? Perhaps she hopes he will fall in love with her mind on the phone and forget she tricked him with some slick camera work. Wrong. That's just not cool. Nobody likes being misled. Nobody likes being lied to. It's unfair and it's uncomfortable, and it can be expensive, exasperating, and irritating. And there is another thought to consider. There are a lot of men out there who would want a larger woman! (Or whatever other insecurity that you have.) Hiding who you are may prevent you from finding the person who will appreciate you for all of the qualities you possess. Generally, I saw men be gracious and kind. I heard from many of them that they went out on the date even though they were disappointed. They remained calm, relaxed, and collected even though they felt cheated. Not all men are nice, but nice men are lovely.

Women are not the only ones who are misleading on

dating sites. Several men lied about their ages by five to ten years. It was frustrating to me, as I was honest. I have cared for myself and don't look my age. I have been doing Bikram Yoga (105 degrees in the hot room for ninety minutes) for over twenty years. I eat well and have a juicer on my counter to make fresh, green vegetable juice. My home has a water filtration system, so I drink clean, pure water daily. I eat well, and I love to cook delicious, healthy food. Fitness is important to me. I wanted to find someone who valued his health the way I did.

    I gave a twelve-year window on my profile and was willing to date men aged forty-eight to sixty. Many sixty-five to seventy-year-old men pretended to be sixty, then told the truth when we talked. I was disappointed and wondered what else they were lying about. Additionally, I met a lot of men who showed up looking much older than their pictures. That wasn't very pleasant. Many of the men I met in person were drinkers and had big red noses to prove it. Other men looked as though they had never owned a bottle of sunscreen! My final thought here—the truth is good enough. Be radically honest. Show yourself the way you are. It will serve you.

PROFILE HINTS

- Let people see who you are. Share something personal. Be vulnerable. If your life hasn't been perfect, it's OK. Nobody has had an ideal life. But don't overdo it. Many people loathe drama and want to meet a person who is happy, well-adjusted, and fun!
- Proofread your profile. I only sent correspondence if a profile contained fewer than two grammatical or spelling errors. I wanted someone who could speak well and had put time and effort into creating the profile.
- If it feels right, share your philosophy on life. I liked it when a profile had a picture of the book a man was reading or a particular painting or sculpture that inspired him. I enjoyed seeing words of wisdom he lived by or some unique saying he resonated with that set him apart from the others. Here are some I remember reading:

> "Life is what happens to you while you're busy making other plans" -Allen Saunders

> *"Only look back to see how far you have come"* -Winnie the Pooh
>
> *"Lessons in life will be repeated until they are learned"* -Frank Sonnenberg
>
> *"I just want a hand to hold, eyes which listen, and a heart which understands"* -Karen Salmansohn
>
> *"The greatest gift you can give somebody is your own personal development"* - Jim Rohn

It was obvious if a profile was thrown together in ten minutes. I wasn't impressed and spent little time there.

CHOOSING PROFILE PHOTOS

Your photos reveal more than the color of your eyes, hair, and skin. They should capture your personality and give a snapshot of your life. I could get a feel for a person's energy by looking through eight or ten pictures. If you are a happy person, be sure you are smiling. If you walk or hike alone in nature, a picture would be a great way to show where you have been. If you are social, include pictures with people around you. You can post a picture with your kids if you are a parent. If you have your parents, posting a picture with them might be fun.

Many pictures are better than fewer. I loved profiles

with at least ten pictures that told a story of a man's life. I wanted to see if he was active. Did he like cycling, hiking, camping, traveling, eating out, exercising, or reading? I wanted to know if he had family and friends. Nothing looks bleaker than a man or woman alone in fifteen photos. I wanted to see if a man showed his eyes and his smile. I wanted to know if he had nice teeth and friendly eyes. I was interested in the clothes that he wore and the way he posed for pictures. You can learn a LOT if you take the time to see what is being shared.

Don't choose photos that are too far away or blurry. And if there are multiple people in the picture, make sure it's clear which one you are. It was challenging when there was a group in the photo, and I had to figure out who was writing the profile.

Include full body shots and realistic renditions. Men told me they were frustrated when a woman took photos of only their upper half. Both men and women asked, again and again, if the photos were current and representative.

I had some hard-and-fast profile photo rules after dating for a few months:

- No smile? No interest. I never take a picture without smiling, and I love to see a man's teeth!

- I didn't reach out if I couldn't see the eyes. It was shocking to me that men took profile pictures with sunglasses on. I assumed the man was hiding something if I couldn't see his eyes. Either that or he was too shy for me.
- If I saw alcohol in multiple pictures, I didn't make contact. I wasn't interested in getting hung up with a man who liked alcohol more than he liked me.
- Dress the way you want to be perceived. It seems obvious, but it has been shocking seeing the photos people put out there on their profiles. I know a woman who is conservative, religious, and looking for a monogamous, long-term relationship. She seeks a gentleman who will treat her with respect and kindness. Her photos will not attract such a man. She looks like she is interested in a one-night stand. She is scantily clad in her photos and wears a smile that invites trouble. Had I known her better, I would have shared my thoughts. She didn't ask me, so I didn't volunteer. It's easy to show your shape without being half-naked. A gentleman will appreciate you leaving a little bit to his imagination.

I was baffled by the number of profiles donning men without shirts, minus the reason to be shirtless. Some men were shirtless for every photo, and I decided they were all brawn and no brain. Yuk. Too much skin in the pictures was a turnoff for me. A tasteful chest photo is certainly welcomed if a man is sailing, swimming, or at the beach. That said, a selfie taken in a dark bathroom in the mirror is weird and creepy. I did have some laughs on my journey to Mr. Right. Keeping a healthy sense of humor as you navigate your way to love is helpful.

- Only photos and no words? No, thank you.
- No body shot, no contact.

A profile should give a clear vision of who you are. It should reflect your values, interests, hopes, dreams, and deal-breakers, and share some of your history. I loved a profile that could make me laugh or feel emotion. Put some energy and thought into building your profile, and you will have better luck attracting what you want. One last thing—for goodness' sake, don't build a profile full of selfies! I cannot tell you how many men took selfies shooting up with the camera so that I was looking into their nostrils! (And many kept their glasses on too.) Take some decent pictures. Be sure they are clear. Show your eyes and your smile.

THE FINISHING TOUCH

Finally, ask a few friends, both men and women, to review your profile and make suggestions. Choose people you trust and who care about you and have what you want—a healthy, happy relationship. Ask them to be honest with you. Ask them to describe the way they see you in your profile. Ask them if the person in the profile represents the person they have come to know and love. Be open to their ideas. Listen without interruption and take time to consider their opinions. If necessary, set another time to talk to gain insight and clarity, but first wait twenty-four hours to reflect. Be sure you ask about the photos you have included. Make sure they are flattering and representative. Don't be attached to their opinion. Listen, learn, and thank them for their time and advice.

Invest time and energy in your profile. It will pay you back.

Chapter Three
MY PROFILE

Below is the profile I used while finding my match. I hope that you find it helpful!

I am an enthusiastic entrepreneur mother of two adult boys and have been divorced for three years. I am not looking for anyone to take care of me. I am high-energy and love to have fun and travel. I have time and the finances to travel often and am looking for someone who has the same. I love to laugh, eat, and try new things. I would love to meet an open, curious man who loves to talk and listen. I love to have deep conversations, and I have done my inner work. I am looking for someone confident and humble who has had some hard knocks and has come out the other side with strength, courage, and humility.

Gratitude is my pathway, and I seek someone who finds the good in each situation.

I love a man who is gracious to everyone he meets, whether it be the restaurant's waiter, the hotel's gardener, or the homeless man on the street. I love a great smile and someone who can laugh at himself. I gravitate toward confidence but not ego.

I am physically fit and hope to meet someone for whom exercise is essential. I love cycling, yoga, hiking, and walking on the beach. I am originally from Colorado and love the mountains and the ocean. Being in nature soothes me, and I love the solar system. I am mesmerized by the moon, the sun, the stars, and the sunset.

I have done much work on myself and love to read and write. I have read Eckhart Tolle, Marianne Williamson, Debbie Ford, Caroline Myss, Wayne Dyer, and Joe Dispenza, to name a few. I would love to hang out with someone who likes to read, even together at times, and who has a creative streak in him. I have written a book on Amazon, and I have a few more in me. I love a man who can speak well and has good grammar.

Trust, monogamy, and loyalty are essential to me. I love chivalry and have taught my boys how to treat a woman. I love when someone opens a door for me, and I enjoy spending time with a gentleman. I work hard to show my partner that I value him :)

I am drawn to nontraditional and have always said that if ninety-nine people go one way, I will probably go the other. I used to think that wasn't a good thing. Now I am grateful. I love a wise man, and I strive to gain wisdom myself!

I can enjoy any date. I love to drink coffee or green juice on a patio on a sunny day. I love to walk on the beach and read together under an umbrella. I love to work out together and have a meal. I love to dress up and go out to dinner. I love a concert at Red Rocks Amphitheatre in Colorado. I love Zion National Park, Monument Valley, Bryce Canyon, and Yosemite. I love to cycle early in the morning in any of these places! It's my dream to go to Australia with a man I'm passionate about. I would love to visit India and New Zealand and cycle in the French or Italian countryside. I don't care what I do when I am with a person who can make me laugh!

I am sexually healthy. I love to hold hands and have no problem showing affection in public.

I love a man who enjoys kids and animals and has a healthy relationship with social media, technology, and alcohol. I'm not looking for perfect, just perfect for me.

Chapter Four
CONNECTING

SCANNING THE PROFILES

Finding your match is like looking for a job. The process is the same. If you were looking for work, you would scan the ads, see what's available, listen to your gut, and take action. You'd consider the time slots you have during the week, and would reserve time to review the options, reach out and make contact, and follow up. Consistency is the key.

Before you click through the profiles, I encourage you to review the scraps of paper in your second vessel. Do this a few times a week. Just run through them quickly, imagining the feelings of already having what you want, and be sure you are feeling good. This way, you land in the perfect space to attract your desired match. Remember, the "who you need to become" vessel is equally important. Working on yourself to become the person who can attract what you want is key.

MAKING CONTACT

There are a few dating sites where the woman reaches out to the man. I preferred any equal opportunity site where either of us could initiate contact. I liked the idea of a man looking at my photos, deciding there was some energy in them that he wanted, formulating a "hello," and making contact. I also liked the freedom of flipping through the photos a man chose to put forward, reading the words he used to describe himself and his life, and taking the initiative with a short note.

My correspondence always began with a compliment. People need to get more compliments. Just ask them. I commented on their eyes, their smile, their energy, or something in their photos that grabbed my attention. I wanted them to know that there was something specific that drew me to them. I usually said, "I like your smile and energy. Call me if you'd like to talk," or "You have kind eyes and a warm smile. Call me if you are interested in a conversation." I was comfortable with leaving my number, and I always did. However, I asked them to text me first so I could make myself available or set up a time to talk on the phone. Man or woman, you may not feel comfortable giving out your information. If you are concerned about your safety and privacy, you might consider getting a separate phone number so you are not giving out your personal one. Many men told me, "I'm sick of texting and emailing. I'm busy, and so are women. I want to meet and see if there's any chemistry." Men were frustrated that getting a date took too much time and effort. They were eager to get together in person. Nearly every man I spoke to was pleasantly surprised that I took the direct approach and put my number out there on the first contact. Here's the truth. I could've texted and emailed, gone back and forth for days, and felt an excellent connection. Then, I could've met the man in person and discovered there was no chemistry. Instead, I chose not to get my hopes up or invest valuable time and energy before meeting in person—end of story.

Here's how I did it. The man would either respond to me inside the dating app or text me. Keeping track of who they were was challenging since I corresponded with multiple people. I would immediately look them up or ask for their "handle" to figure it out. I reread their profile and added their number to my phone with "dating app" in the name. For example, I would say "David from Laguna Beach" and "dating app" for the last name. I would add all their profile details to the "Notes." I usually used the voice feature on my phone so I didn't have to type. I wanted to know all about them before we connected so that I could ask good questions, comment on their photos, and remember what grabbed my attention in the first place. I was eager to put a "no" next to the last name or set a meeting time. I learned a lot from these phone calls. Let me share some of my findings.

I liked a man who took control of the conversation. I liked it when a man commented on something about my profile. I wanted him to notice the photos of my boys, my smile, or the fact that I was a cyclist. It was a good sign that he was observant and interested in me. I made it my business to be interested in him as well. I commented on his children, his interests, and his photos. I asked questions and listened attentively for clues. I learned that many men talked and talked and never asked me a question. They were either self-absorbed or nervous. Either way, they were not for me. I heard, again and again, that women were the same. They rambled on about former husbands, children, and hobbies without asking a single question. Yikes. Being excited to learn about another seems pretty elementary, but evidently, it's not. My mom always says, "I know my own story. I'm excited to learn about someone else's!" It makes sense to me. It comes down to the Golden Rule—treat others as you want to be treated. And, if you want to be interesting, be interested!

I remember a man called me while I was driving to meet another man for coffee. I had a fifteen-minute drive. He said, "Hello, is this Carrie?" I said three words —"Yes, it is." He talked and talked and never took a breath. Finally, there was a long pause and he said, "Are you there?" I said, "Yes. I'm here, but I don't think you and I have enough in common to meet in person." He said, "I don't know why this keeps happening to me!" I said, "Are you aware that you just talked for thirteen minutes and forty-nine seconds, and I never said a word? You may be a very nice man, but how would I know?" He was flustered and likely a bit embarrassed. I wished him good luck and hung up. I have heard that women are also guilty of not being interested enough to ask questions. And if they do, they rarely listen to the answer. Instead, they use the answer as an opportunity to turn the conversation back to themselves. It's a sickness, and we all need better training. It's common courtesy to be curious. You can learn a lot about a person in a concise amount of time by listening for clues. Why not save yourself an hour, an evening, and a few bucks by showing interest, probing, searching for clarity, and asking another question? It's just intelligent dating!

Here's why I was so excited to listen to a man. I was

on a mission to find my partner. I wasn't looking for a free meal (I think that's pretty lame) or to fill an evening. I had plenty to do, and I could buy my own food. I was going through the numbers, just like in my sales career. I could learn a lot by talking on the phone, and I was determined to find out, in as short a time as possible, whether or not there would be a date. I made it my business to follow my gut.

Here's what I looked for. I wanted a man who had been a husband and a father. This way, we would have more in common. I wanted a man with a positive outlook who had been through some "stuff" and was willing to talk about it. He needed to be confident and secure without being cocky. I wanted a man who was open and enthusiastic about life and possibility. If I heard about spontaneity in his life, that excited me. I usually asked a man about his dating experiences, which told me a lot! Some men were hesitant to share, and I encouraged them. I would ask, "So, tell me, how long have you been on the dating site, and how do you like it?" I would ask, "How did you end up on the site in the first place?" or "How often do you have a date?" It's not the answer I'm looking for. I'm interested in what I can learn about them from the response. I have had men tell me horror stories, and I loved hearing how they handled themselves. For example, a man told me he showed up to find that his prospective match was at least sixty pounds heavier than her pictures portrayed. Surprised and disappointed, he said, "I tried to hide my frustration and took her to dinner because I'm a gentleman." I was impressed. Others gave me similar anecdotes and told me they left the woman at the door.

Here are some of my conversation starters. Take what works and leave the rest. I'm not attached!

- How long have you been dating online?
- How did you come to make a profile?
- How has your dating experience been thus far?
- Were you born and raised here, or did you relocate at some point?
- What do you like to do for fun?
- Do you have children?
- Do you have any pets?
- What kind of movies do you like?
- What kind of food do you like?
- Do you eat to live or live to eat? (I live to eat!)
- Are you an early riser or a night owl?
- What is on your bucket list?
- Do you enjoy reading?
- Where did you go on your last trip?
- Do you have siblings? Where are they located? Are you close with them?

- What is your favorite holiday?

There were two things that most men repeatedly mentioned when I asked about their time on dating sites. First, they told me it took too long to get to the date and meet a woman in person. They were tired of communicating virtually and wished they could meet more women without all the up-front pomp and circumstance. I felt the same way. Second, they told me that they were tired of the drama. They wanted a woman who was relatively stable and happy. They had already been through some anguish and pain with their situations and were looking to move forward with a well-adjusted and cheerful partner. That sounded good to me!

When I first got on the site, I second-guessed myself. I suggested a phone call even when there was something inconsistent in a man's profile. I would meet him out of FOMO (fear of missing out) rather than because I was drawn to his energy on the phone. I agreed to a second date a few times even though I was 90 percent sure there wouldn't be a third one. I was in constant fear of leaving something on the table. I feared making a mistake. What I failed to remember is that God was in control.

Let's cut to the chase here. I learned how to

streamline the process and helped men do the same. We usually talked for fifteen to thirty minutes. It was long enough for me to understand who they were. Sometimes I would get on the phone with a man and know almost immediately that there wasn't a connection. Rather than try to explain why and risk hurting his feelings unnecessarily, I would cut the conversation short and suggest we talk again soon. I would follow up a day or two later with a voice message telling him I didn't feel energy beyond friendship. I never kept anyone hanging.

THE ONE-HOUR GIRL

If I was interested in getting together, I would say it. "You sound like a nice guy. Let's meet in person. Would you be up for it?" If they agreed, I shared my thoughts about what a first date should look like. I told them, "I'm excited to meet you, and I have to tell you I have become the 'one-hour' girl. I want to meet for juice or a cup of coffee and talk for an hour. You don't even have to buy my juice or coffee. I want to meet and see if we are interested in getting together again. After talking for a bit, we can say goodbye. If one of us reaches out after the initial meeting, we can agree there was chemistry. If not, we can move forward and only spend a little time, energy, and money. Is this OK with you?"

For the most part, they were thrilled. Men were

tired of spending their valuable money on dinners and costly activities, especially when they immediately knew there was no connection. I knew at "hello" whether I would want to see a man again. It was in the way he looked, the way he dressed, and how he greeted me. It was in his smile and his eyes. I felt it or did not. And mostly, I did not. And that was OK! I didn't want to spend more than an hour (and sometimes would have preferred a lot less time) asking questions, listening attentively, and pretending I was assessing the situation when it was clear we wouldn't see each other again. I was already feeling disappointment in my heart. I was usually ready to move on very quickly. Many men felt the same way.

I saved myself and others countless hours and dollars by adhering to my one-hour rule, which eventually dropped to forty-five minutes. After eight months of being the "one-hour girl," I became the "forty-five-minute girl." It felt so much better. And don't misunderstand. There were a few times when I would have gone on a second date. The man didn't call me back. And that's OK. I didn't take it personally (well, maybe a little) and moved on. Let's face it. Most dates are going to go nowhere. It's true. Why not streamline the process and reduce the sting of rejection a little bit or a lot?

You might conclude that I didn't give men a chance

or take the time to get to know them. I completely understand that line of thinking. However, I am a firm believer in following my gut. My heart knew what I wanted, and I made it my business to listen. I left the rest up to God and the universe.

Chapter Five
THE DATE

Upon meeting me, men would usually make a joke like, "Well, we had better get to a table and start talking fast. We only have another fifty-seven minutes!" It was a great way to break the ice, showing men my time was valuable. It also showed them I honored their time and wanted to use it wisely. I rarely broke the one-hour rule. I had a lot of first dates. I knew what I wanted and would know him when I found him.

It's important to suggest meeting in a public place where both parties feel safe and comfortable. I chose coffee shops, juice bars, or outdoor patios. It depended on the day of the week, the time, and the weather. I preferred meeting in the afternoon, as making it a shorter meeting was easy. I loved it when a man took control and gave me an idea about where to meet and when. I was ready and willing to choose a meeting time and place if a man asked me to. I suggest you simplify the process by considering a few ideas before making contact.

There were other reasons why I liked to meet at places where we could order, receive our juice or coffee, and start the conversation right away. It was simple, and I had better control of the situation, as did my date. I didn't ever want to be at the mercy of a lagging waiter or a long line at a restaurant with a waiting list. As a man, I would not be comfortable opening myself up to a huge bill or a long meal at a mediocre restaurant with a woman I had no interest in seeing again. Just sayin'.

Upon meeting a man, I smiled brightly and usually hugged him. Remember, the person you meet is just as nervous as you are, and you can put them at ease. I usually said, "Thank you for being on time" or "Thank you for taking the time to meet me." Many times I would find a way to compliment a man. "Nice smile!" or "I like your shoes! I love it when a man wears something other than flip-flops or sneakers." I let a man initiate the ordering process, but was always willing and ready to pay. It was polite to offer. Men appreciated the gesture, although I never insisted. If they took control and paid for my juice or coffee, I was grateful and always thanked them. Further, I told them that I didn't expect it. If they held the door for me or pulled out my chair, I said something like, "Thank you! Chivalry isn't dead in the state of California!"

I made it my business to be a good conversationalist. I asked questions and listened with interest. I tried to be present with their answers and commented from time to time. I was open, willing to share my journey, and interested in learning about theirs. I remember when men were anxious and uncomfortable discussing their past situations. It was important to me to have someone who was relatively healed and who had been out of a relationship for more than a minute. The concept of taking a year or two to reflect attracted me.

After about twenty-five dates, I had my system down. I checked the site several times a day. I responded promptly. I reached out and made connections. I followed up. I worked hard to have short phone conversations. I made myself available for the mini-dates. I learned not to be attached. And I had success. More on that later.

Chapter Six

WHEN THE SPARKS DON'T FLY

After the date, I sent a voice text or message. I wanted men to hear the sincerity in my voice. I thanked every man for spending his valuable time and energy meeting me. I gave him a sincere compliment. I commented on something I learned about him on our date and wished him well in the future. I would write it out if I couldn't leave a voice text.

An unexpected benefit of my online dating experience was learning to tell the truth. I learned to be completely honest during the fourteen months I was on the site. My messages went something like this:

"Hey, Matt, this is Carrie from the dating site. Thank you so much for sharing your valuable time with me this afternoon. You are a smart, accomplished man, and I enjoyed our time together. I loved hearing about your mountain biking adventures and the funny encounters you have had. While you will be a perfect match for another woman, I didn't feel much beyond friendship when we were together today. I wish you all good things in the future because you deserve them. All the best to you!"

"Hey, Michael! It's Carrie from the dating site. Listen, thank you for your time this morning. I appreciated you getting together with me on the spur of the moment. I have to be honest with you. I talked for about fifteen minutes of the one hour we spent together. I recognize that you may have been nervous, but I am only mentioning this so that you can be aware of it for your next date. I loved learning about your kids and your business and would love to have shared some details about my life. You are a great father and a smart businessman. I know you will find the woman you are looking for. Again, all the best to you, and thank you for your time today!"

"Hey, Jake. It's Carrie from the dating site. We met this afternoon. First, thank you for the juice and for treating me like a lady. I appreciated your ordering for me, asking them to turn the music down a little so we could talk, and walking me to my car. You are a true gentleman. I felt like you were guarded when you talked about your previous marriage. It seemed like you were still angry and bitter. It felt like you had some things to sort out and still had one foot back in that situation. You are a handsome man with a lot going for you. I hope you will find this assessment to be helpful and not hurtful. You deserve to be happy. Thank you again for meeting me today, and best of luck to you."

"Hey, Brad, it's Carrie from the dating site. Thank you for your time this afternoon. Also, thank you for the latte! You are an adorable daddy and a wise and gracious man. I enjoyed getting to know you a little bit today. That said, you and I are at different stages of our lives. I am a double-empty nester, as my boys are on their journeys while you are still raising those beautiful young girls. I am at the point in my life where I have the freedom to go and to do, and I am looking for a man who has the same. Let women know you are raising the kids and share fifty-fifty custody. It certainly will not be a deterrent for all women out there. I have friends who would love to meet a man with children, as they have been unable to bear their own. Again, thank you for your time, and best of luck to you, Brad!"

You get the idea. I was honest with men. I told them why I wasn't interested in another date. I hoped to help them find what they were looking for. I appreciated it when they gave me suggestions and ideas on what I could do better. Online dating is hard. It takes courage, time, and energy. The least I could do was be open and generous and share my ideas on how they could improve the odds of meeting their match online.

Chapter Seven

A FEW OF MY DATES

I have had some funny stuff happen on my short dates with men. Here are a few of the more memorable ones.

Date A: I meet the man at an outdoor café for wine. He is handsome, well-dressed, and on time. Good start. We talk for about thirty minutes. He fails to have eye contact even one time. He looks everywhere else but at me. He tells me he has been dating online for quite some time. He shares that he has a son and doesn't need a woman around since he has already had his kids. He is detached and doesn't seem very interested in me. I ask, "Charles, you are a handsome man. You were on time and well-dressed, and I was excited to meet you. Do you know you haven't looked at me once in forty-five minutes? You have been cold and distant and seem to have little interest in having a woman in your life. I'm not sure why we are here together." He is shocked. He spends the next fifteen minutes meeting my eyes and trying to connect but the moment has passed. I imagine he has been hurt before, and his walls are built high. I'm not interested in going further with him. I thank him for his time and wish him well. I am incredibly grateful that I don't have to sit there for an entire dinner. Yikes!

Date B: A man asks me to meet him at a gorgeous restaurant patio in Laguna Beach. It's been raining for a week, so I assume we will sit under an umbrella and it won't be busy. One hour before the date, the sky clears, the sun comes out, and it's gorgeous! I will have to hustle to get to the restaurant on time to get parked, inside, and, hopefully, get a table. My date never gets that far in his thinking. He shows up fourteen minutes late without a text letting me know he is on the way. Before the date, he asks if my pictures are current and representative of my appearance. I assure him that they are and figure that I'll get the same courtesy. Nope. Not at all. He walks in with a twenty-five-pound paunch leading the way and tells me he is nursing a hangover. He orders a Coke, and I tell him I must go to the bathroom. I consider walking out the front door but can't bring myself to be that rude. Instead, I join him at the table and ask him if I can be frank with him. He says I can. I say, "Neil. You live just up the road from here in Newport Beach. I live just south of here in San Juan

Capistrano. You and I know how crazy busy Laguna Beach is in the summer. When I saw the sunrise today, I moved quickly to get parked, get to the restaurant on time, and put our name on the list for a patio table. You told me yesterday you were excited to meet me. If I were a man eager to meet a woman, I would have gotten here early, picked a lovely table on the patio, and texted her where I was sitting outside. I would have waited for her to walk in, and I would have risen from the table and pulled out her chair. You were fourteen minutes late today. My rule is fifteen minutes and I'm gone. You haven't apologized or attempted to explain why you didn't arrive promptly. You ordered a Coke without offering me anything and didn't think twice about telling me you were hungover."

There is a woman named Mary Kay Ash, the founder of Mary Kay Cosmetics, who taught me something I use in my business and life. It goes like this: "Pretend that every single person you meet has a sign around his or her neck that says, 'Make me feel important.'" "Neil, you have not made me feel important today. I'm going to leave now and go to the beach. Good luck to you." I walk out and never look back. I was in my late fifties, and I know a lot has changed over the last few decades, but common sense doesn't seem that common anymore. Gentlemen, a little bit of chivalry goes a long way. And women? Be gracious and show gratitude when a man extends himself and treats you like a lady. And for heaven's sake, act like one too.

Note: Recently, my mom got me a shirt for my birthday that reads, "Underestimate me. That will be fun." I don't wear it but hang it on my office wall. I really like it.

Date C: I drive forty-five minutes to meet a busy and handsome mortgage broker for lunch. He is so busy he doesn't eat. He is surprised that I am on time, happy, successful, and emotionally available. I order and eat my healthy salad. I laugh at his jokes. I have a few funny dating stories to tell. I share a little about my boys and business and am excited to hear about his life. In the thirty minutes, I learn that he is separated and still living with his wife. He is afraid to leave her high and dry because she has been the surrogate mother for his twelve-year-old son for five years. He admits he married her because he needed a wife and she seemed nice. She faces serious surgery, and he plans to support her through it. Never mind that she is an alcoholic and drinks daily in front of his son. She got drunk a few months before our lunch date. They were with friends on an outdoor patio in Laguna Beach and she started a fight with a man with whom she did not align politically. My date jumped in to defend his drunk wife, got physical with the intoxicated man, and both were arrested. My date is in the middle of settling the matter with the law. Wow. That was a lot to follow! I feel lucky when I drive home that day. I am free. I am unencumbered. I have dealt with a ton of my stuff and have moved forward.

This man could have benefited greatly by reading Chapter Two of this book, especially the part entitled "Clean up." What on earth was this dude doing on a dating site in the first place? He was terrified of being alone. He was looking for the next woman to fill his cup and needed to fill his own. Here's the moral of this story, and I have said it before. If you don't do your work, you may attract the mate of your dreams, and you won't be ready to receive them. This man continues to contact me for months after our date. He is such a good man. He is successful, friendly, handsome, and intelligent. I might have been interested in him if he had cleaned up his life and left time for his wounds to heal before meeting me online.

Here are the final four words on this point: Do your inner work. It's important. It's fair. It's kind.

Chapter Eight
RESOURCES AND INSPIRATION

I want to share a few books and concepts that helped me on my dating journey and in life. I promise they will help you if you are open. The first of these is *The Four Agreements*, by Don Miguel Ruiz. While all four agreements are phenomenal, two are essential in finding your match online. They are:

- Don't take anything personally.
- Don't make assumptions.

I will say little about these two agreements because it would be impossible for me to do better than Ruiz did in his book. It is a must-read for anyone. I encourage you to order it right away. It will serve you and everyone with whom you come in contact. Dating can be tough on the ego, especially if you have been out of the arena for years or even decades. It is beneficial to internalize that we each have a particular pair of lenses through which we see ourselves and others. We each come to the table with unique experiences, wounds, and baggage. Exploring the above concepts can help us navigate the online dating journey.

Another book that has been of tremendous help to me is *The Wisdom of the Enneagram*, by Don Richard Riso and Russ Hudson. You may have learned of personality profiling (Myers-Briggs Type Indicator and The Big Five, to name a couple) concerning the workplace. The Enneagram is more spiritual. There are nine personality types, including the Reformer, the Helper, The Achiever, The Individualist, the Investigator, the Loyalist, the Enthusiast, the Challenger, and the Peacemaker. Each type has unique qualities and characteristics, and the book is an excellent examination of how each functions. This book set me free. After determining I was a seven on the Enneagram, I read about my type's healthy, average, and unhealthy versions. I discovered some challenges I face being wired the way I am. I began to understand why I am the way I am. I learned about my strengths, weaknesses, innate patterns, and behaviors. My awareness of them gave me the ability to recognize and transform them. What a gift this book has given me in understanding why I do what I do, act the way I act, and feel the way I feel. It is difficult to change what you're not aware of. I cannot say enough about how this book has given me a better understanding of myself, my children, my parents, my extended family members, and my co-entrepreneurs. It is an incredible tool that I cannot recommend highly enough.

The Big Leap, by Gay Hendricks, is an incredible read for anyone striving to be the best version of themselves in business, personal relationships, and love. Hendricks teaches about the zones of incompetence, competence, excellence, and genius. He explores the concepts of self-sabotage and "upper limiting" as we strive for more success in these areas. Over the years, I have read this book many times. I am reading it as I write these words, and it is sincerely helping me to identify and dissipate some of my self-limiting behaviors in my love relationship.

A concept that has been of tremendous help to me on my personal development journey is shadow work. "The shadow" is a term coined by psychologist Carl Jung. Shadow work is identifying, recognizing, and owning those parts of ourselves that we'd rather ignore, repress, or deny. Often, we can easily spot these negative characteristics in other people and fail to see them in ourselves. We react strongly to anger, greed, and judgment in others and may fail to recognize them in ourselves. When we can shine the light on the dark places inside us, we can become whole and free. I'm still determining if I will ever finish doing my shadow work, but I am grateful to know about it, and it has undoubtedly helped me to understand why I do what I do. Shadow work is a blessing to you and to those who come in contact with you—enough said.

I love something Marianne Williamson shared many years ago when I attended a service at the Church of Today in Warren, Michigan, where she was the senior minister. Marianne said, "I'm not depressed by the gap between Jesus and me because I am so impressed by the gap between Jesus and me I used to be!" I laughed my head off when she said this, and I still find it incredibly amusing today. Wow! She is a brilliant woman, and I adore her books and teachings. I especially love *A Woman's Worth*. It should be required reading for all young women as they go through puberty.

Gary Chapman has written a book called *The 5 Love Languages*. This book is a quick and easy read and quite enjoyable. It can be hugely valuable when entering the dating game. The five love languages are physical touch, receiving gifts, acts of service, words of affirmation, and quality time. Knowing your primary love language and the love language of the person you are dating can provide much insight.

The Work of Byron Katie (www.thework.com) is a

fantastic way to overcome negative thoughts that may threaten your confidence level, self-esteem, and success in finding your partner. I recommend familiarizing yourself with the four questions and the turnaround to help you navigate online dating with dignity, determination, poise, and certainty.

One of my favorite motivational speakers of all time is Jim Rohn. I resonate deeply with his philosophy on life. Jim says, "The greatest gift you can give somebody is your own personal development. I used to say, 'If you will take care of me, I will take care of you.' Now I say, 'I will take care of me for you, if you will take care of you for me.'" If you work hard to become the person you want to attract, you will have a greater chance of finding your match online.

Chapter Nine
LAST THOUGHTS

Be Safe. Use caution in every way. Nothing weird happened while I was on my online dating journey but I have certainly heard stories. Any way you crack it, you are meeting a stranger. Think carefully about where you should be meeting someone you don't know. Meeting in a public place is wise. Having other people around is not only safe but generally much more comfortable. Limit the personal information you share when meeting someone for the first time. Only volunteer a little about your financial situation, the location of your office, or specific details about your family members. Keeping the first date short will help. You will be less likely to say too much if your time together is limited.

Be Patient. Be smart. Take your time. If it's good today, it will be good in six months. If it's good in six months, it will be good in two years. There shouldn't be any rush. You will be more likely to choose well if you are in decent shape physically, financially, emotionally, and spiritually. If you are young, take the time to figure out who you are and what you want before looking to partner with another. If you have taken the time to heal from your divorce, spouse's death, or breakup, you will make better choices.

Recently, I was walking my puppy, Archie. I met a woman who told me quite a horror story. She had met a man online who was, of course, good-looking and incredible initially. This woman had money and property and had invested in the market. They married just months after their first date. When her husband was done with her seven years later, she had nothing left. I didn't get many details, but I certainly got the gist of the story. She admitted that the signs were there. She had missed them. She was lonely, wounded, and anxious to find a partner. Be patient. There is no rush. And if you feel rushed, I encourage you to ask yourself why. Needy people do not make good partners. I should know. I have been one.

Be Intentional. From beginning to end, be aware. It all starts with your choice of a dating site. There are many out there from which to choose. If you are a woman and want to choose a man, Bumble is an option. If you are more visual and want to swipe left for the "no's" and right for the "yeses," then Plenty of Fish might work best for you. I am a huge believer in physical chemistry. I don't consider it wrong to "judge a book by its cover" in this situation. If you are verbal, love to communicate, are a bit older and are set in your ways, eharmony may be the best choice. My advice is to be clear about what you want, why you want it, and what you are willing to do to get it. Be ready to compromise, learn, and use good common sense. Whether you are a man or woman, set intentions as you navigate your dating journey.

Be Fearless. Being in a relationship with another is the fast track to personal development. Be open, be gracious, be tolerant, and have empathy. We all have wounds that we haven't yet healed. We have a past and deserve compassion for all we have been through. We attract people who can help us face, address, and release the chains that bind us. Be willing to talk and be ready to listen. Be willing to change but keep who you are in the process. It's a balance.

Author and public speaker Caroline Myss talks about being "shattered" upon our arrival here on earth. The goal of the earthly journey is to gather the pieces of ourselves and put the proverbial "Humpty Dumpty" back together again. As you engage with another, you may receive a valuable part of yourself that they have brought. Everyone you meet has something to teach you.

Each person carries a piece of your puzzle for integration.

Be Yourself. Everyone else is taken. Be bold and show who you are from the onset. If you don't like to camp, don't go camping because your potential partner likes it. If you want to drink a lot, do not rein it in. Avoid the bait-and-switch technique. Trust me—many people out there will be happy to party it up with you! If you dislike exercising, don't put on the spandex and attempt to impress. Don't pretend you are an early riser if you like to sleep in. If you fake it, you will not make it in this case. It only causes heartbreak, for you or another.

Be Kind. Adhere to the Golden Rule. Do unto others as you would have them do unto you. Treat others the way you wish to be treated. Be the change you'd like to see in the world.

In closing, I would like to share one of my favorite quotes from Winnie the Pooh: "You are braver than you believe, stronger than you seem, smarter than you think, and loved more than you will ever know." You can do this dating thing. You can find what you are looking for if you are willing to expend some time and effort. And remember, the harder you work at it, the luckier you will be. I believe in you. Reach out or respond to new people every day with love in your heart. You may not get exactly what you want from online dating, but you will get what you need.

At the time of this writing, I have fallen in love. Jay treats me the way I have yearned to be treated. I am learning how to listen with the intention of hearing. I am learning how to be a partner and what it feels like to have one. Time with Jay is bringing my core principles into sharp focus. We are exploring our values to see how they align. I have recovered many pieces of the puzzle called Carrie Crane Dickie. I am so blessed and grateful for all I am learning as I navigate this life as part of a couple.

IF THIS BOOK WAS HELPFUL TO YOU...

Please leave a review on Amazon.com. Reviews are very valuable to authors.

ABOUT THE AUTHOR

Carrie Dickie's life underwent a profound transformation after a 26-year marriage and raising two adult sons. Despite extraordinary business success, she grappled with inner emptiness, spurring her journey of self-discovery through online dating.

Carrie faced numerous challenges and learned the value of honesty and transparency. Through this process, she uncovered her inner strength, resilience, and renewed self.

Carrie now finds joy in her thriving business, writing, and deep connections with her grown sons and family. In picturesque Orange County, California, the ocean serves as a source of solace and inspiration. Carrie's story exemplifies the power of self-discovery and personal growth in overcoming adversity and finding fulfillment.

www.ingramcontent.com/pod-product-compliance
Lightning Source LLC
Chambersburg PA
CBHW051349040426
42453CB00007B/478